50
AFRICAN AMERICAN
AUDITION
MONOLOGUES

50
AFRICAN AMERICAN
AUDITION
MONOLOGUES

Gus Edwards

HEINEMANN
Portsmouth, NH

Heinemann
A division of Reed Elsevier Inc.
361 Hanover Street
Portsmouth, NH 03801–3912
www.heinemanndrama.com

Offices and agents throughout the world

Performance rights information can be found on page 90.

Library of Congress Cataloging-in-Publication Data
Edwards, Gus.
    50 African American audition monologues / Gus Edwards.
        p. cm.
    ISBN 0-325-00457-9 (alk. paper)
        1. Monologues. 2. Acting—Auditions. 3. African Americans—
Drama. I. Title: Fifty African American audition monologues. II. Title.

ᐟ PN2080 .E35 2002
    812'.54—dc21

                                                                2002004347

Editor: Lisa A. Barnett
Production: Vicki Kasabian
Cover design: Joni Doherty
Author photograph: C. Levin
Typesetter: Tom Allen, Pear Graphic Design
Manufacturing: Steve Bernier

Printed in the United States of America on acid-free paper
06 05 04 03 02   VP   1 2 3 4 5

Contents

A Note on Auditions and Auditioning   ix

30 SECONDS TO 1 MINUTE		
Female	*Age*	
He Said, Then I Said	20s	3
Quotes	any age	4
In a Tired City	any age	5
This Room of Mine	20s	6
Waiting My Turn	any age	7
Fools and Dreamers	20s	8
A New Understanding	40s	9
Trust	30s	10
The Big Mistake	30s	11
Never Again	30s	12
Male		
Mr. Nice Guy	20s	13
The Optimist	30s	14
Everybody's Baffled	20s	15
How It Was Back Then	40s	16
The Last Word	30s	17
Dumb or Something	teens	18
The Old Club	50s	19

What Is the Answer?	teens	21
Somebody Cares	40s	22
Dear Mom	20s	24

1½ TO 2 MINUTES

Female

I Used to Dream	30s	27
An Exchange of Glances	30s	29
The Power of Prayer	40s	31
Because I Love Him	20s	33
Appetites and Horses	30s	35
True Love	30s	37
A Woman's Emotions	20s	39
Learning to Love Jazz	any age	41
Parts Unknown	30s	43
With No Clothes On	20s	45

Male

The Quick Thinker	30s	47
No Reason for Tears	30s	49
Insomnia	40s	51
Show Me Your Bills	any age	53
Paying the Price	20s	55
The False Image	30s	57
Quoting Shakespeare	teens	59
Derelict Ravings	20s	61

Bad Medicine and Prayer   40s   63

Hypocrisy   20s   65

2½ TO 3 MINUTES

Female

Freedom to Love   teens   69

Attaching the Blame   40s   72

Hooked on a Feeling   20s   74

Looking Up at Clouds   20s   76

Dangerous Weather Conditions   30s   78

Male

The Preacherman   20s   80

An Almost Perfect World   30s   82

Living in Dorksville   teens   84

A Warning   40s   86

Wondering Out Loud   50s   88

A Note on Auditions and Auditioning

In my life I think I have done 1500 to 2000 auditions. In an effort at trying to make a living as an actor in New York City between the years of 1960 and 1975, I went to every open audition, cattle call, look-see, and stage manager replacement audition I read about (mostly in *Backstage* and *Showbusiness*), heard about through friends and agents, or stumbled into just by chance or dumb luck. These auditions either had me read from a script or bring in an already prepared monologue of one to three minutes long. Sometimes they would require two memorized pieces. One contemporary, one classical. And if they called me back, they'd want to see something else.

So most of my days at that time were spent working (waiting tables in restaurants mostly) and auditioning. And many of my nights were spent reading plays and short stories, looking for monologues I could have at my fingertips in case that special call came my way. The classical stuff was always easy to find. There were lots of paperback editions of Shakespeare's plays or Moliére or Ibsen or Strindberg around. But finding dramatic African American material was difficult. *A Raisin in the Sun, Dutchman,* and a few other standbys were always available. The problem with those is that they were used and reused so many times that agents and casting directors were very tired of them. So the search for fresh audition material was constant with me. I was always reading and xeroxing and memorizing things I thought I could use. This search required countless number of hours and sleepless nights.

Now you would think that after all those years of trying and working I would've learned something about the audition process. Lord knows I had had ample experience and had even read books about "how to audition." But alas, I didn't.

It was only when I stood on the other side of the production table as a playwright and director did I truly find out what auditioning was all about. As an actor I would read the part, prepare myself mentally, and then go in with the idea of knocking them off their feet with my talent and persona. Sometimes I got the job, more often I didn't. And that generally is par for the course.

What I didn't realize, understand, or appreciate is what the audition process is all about. It wasn't until I became a director that I began to see how wrong I had been. I used to go into those auditions thinking that it was all about me and what I was consciously bringing to the occasion. Now I know that it isn't. It is about something completely out of the actor's control. It is about an idea, an image, a concept, a quality, or sometimes even a look. This is what the playwright and/or director visualizes when he or she is writing or reading the script in the quiet atmosphere of their home or study, in preparation for standing the play up on its feet and, in the director's case, orchestrating it to life . . . "Such and such a character is going to look this way, sound this way and react that way. This other character is going to look and sound thus and such." . . . It's all figured out mentally long before the audition process begins. So the audition itself becomes a means of searching for the actor who most closely resembles or matches the ideas and impressions the director or whomever conjured up mentally before they begin seeing people.

If fifty actors audition for the part, the role generally will go to the one who comes closest to fitting that phantom image. Providing, of course, that he or she displays the general range of skills deemed necessary for playing the part.

This is how I've cast 80 to 90 percent of the plays I've directed. The other 10 to 20 percent of the time I've had to change my mind about a character because no one at the various auditions came close to what I had mentally envisioned. Or in some very rare cases an actor came in and auditioned so force-fully or made such bold and terrific choices that I was forced to change the idea I had conceived and adopt this new one. This is the happiest experience one can have when conducting auditions. But as I said before, it is very rare.

What does this all add up to? Some advice to the actor. Don't go in trying to be what you think they're looking for. There's no way for you to know or even guess what that is. So don't even think about it. Just go in and be yourself, *relaxed, prepared,* and *confident.* Those three words are the key to all of it, I think. Being *relaxed* allows your own full and true personality to shine through. *Preparation* means that you can effortlessly glide through your monologue or scene without strain or awkwardness. And the *confident* actor makes everyone in the room feel confident and secure. Now, this doesn't guarantee that you'll get the part. Nothing can guarantee that. But it does mean that you've shown yourself to your best advantage. And that's all anyone can or should ever ask of himself/herself or anyone else. And sometimes even when you don't get the job, this can pay dividends.

Many years ago, one of my acting teachers, William Hickey (he played Prizzi in the 1985 film *Prizzi's Honor*), told this story to his class.

As a young actor he was once called to audition for a play that was going to Broadway. He auditioned, they called him back and he auditioned some more. At a third call back he was auditioned even further. But in the end he didn't get the part. He shrugged it off and went about his way. A little over two years later he was called and offered a part in another play that was to ultimately be produced on Broadway. Since he was a struggling actor without any kind of exploitable name, he assumed that by *offer* they meant *audition.* So he called them back to clarify what was said. They told him that he was being offered the role, not being asked to come down to read or audition. When he got to the office to sign the contract, he was pleased but genuinely puzzled. So he asked them why he was being accorded this honor. Why was he, a no-name actor, being offered this role? It was because of the audition he had done two years before, he was told. He hadn't gotten the part in that play because it was felt that he didn't fit their concept. But his audition and his two subsequent callbacks were so good that the playwright went out and wrote a character in his new play that would fit Hickey's talents like a glove. And that was the reason he was directly being offered the role.

The lesson here is *play it strong, play it simply,* and *play it with truth.* Over the past many years I have been working as a playwright, director and educator. For many years I ran a workshop for actors of color. In class we did monologues, scene study, and worked on audition techniques. Throughout those years the constant cry I heard from students and other aspiring actors was: "Where can I find fresh material for black actors?" It was a question I had constantly asked when I was a young actor, too. So I set out to provide some new material. My first collection, *Monologues on Black Life* (1997), was followed by *More Monologues on Black Life* (2000). And now you're holding *50 African American Audition Monologues.*

This book contains 50 monologues designed specifically as audition pieces for African American actors. They are of various lengths (mostly short) to provide the black actor with material that would suit any audition requirement.

In my other books I've talked about the need for exercise and class material that speaks to and about African Americans and the African American experience and culture. This book of audition monologues is intended to add to that dialogue and bridge that gap.

30 SECONDS TO 1 MINUTE

He Said, Then I Said

Female—mid 20s

The man say to me, "You don't know nothing 'bout music." I say to him, "You don't know nothing 'bout womens." He say to me, "You don't know nothing 'bout life." So I says to him, "You don't know nothing 'bout nothing." So he say to me, "You wanna bet?" And I say, "Sure." Then he say, "What if I take you up to my room, lay you down on my bed, take all your clothes off a you, and then lay myself down on top of you, would you say that I know a little something about life then?" And I said, "I don't know, I'd have to see."

So that's what he did. He took me up to his room and all that other stuff. After it was over, he look at me and said, "Now will you admit I know a little something?" I told him that I thought he knowed a lot. He smiled and we started going out together regular. Now we is husband and wife with a baby on the way. So I guess it prove that he really did know something about life.

You asked me and now I told you. The truth is I really don't know how a girl should go about getting a husband. I only know how I got mine.

Quotes

I want you to listen to this and tell me who said it. "Fools . . . fools . . . shall we their fond pageants see? Lord what fools these mortals be." . . . Here's another one: "O that this too, too solid flesh would melt, thaw and resolve itself into a dew." . . . Or this: "A woman moved, is like a fountain troubled, muddy, ill-seeming, thick, bereft of beauty, and while it is so, none so dry or thirsty will deign to sip, or touch one drop of it." (Brief pause) I got one more for you. . . . "If that the world and love were young,

> And truth in every shepherd's tongue,
> These pretty pleasures might me move
> To live with thee and be thy love."

By this time of course, you guessed who said that. Said all of it. Shakespeare, of course. William Shakespeare of England. Tell me something, is there anything that guy didn't say?

Now what about Mrs. Shakespeare? How did she feel about all this? Why doesn't anybody ever quote her? Didn't she ever talk? Or did she just hang around the house cooking food and having babies? . . . I think it's really, really odd. Nobody ever quotes Mrs. Shakespeare. And you want to know what? She's the one I would really like to hear from.

In a Tired City

Female—any age

So—you go out and walk through the streets of the tired city. Looking for hope. But hope is something that's hard to find. So you look for dreams, but dreams ain't nowhere to be found either.

Then go back to your room, take off your dress, and think about lying down for a while. Cause if you lie down then you might fall asleep. And sleep is the only place where hope and dreams have any kind of chance in this tired city.

Then you change your mind and decide to look out the window one more time at this collection of buildings and streets that pretends it cares. But that's all it is, a game of pretend. Cause it don't really give a damn. Not about anything. Or anyone. It never did, and never will. . . . Not about me, not about you, not about the 9-to-5-ers who go to work every day. Or the holy ones who pray and watch TV every night. They is all lost souls floating in this fish tank we call life. Swimming around in circles, never getting anywhere except to where we been before. Endlessly swimming but not going any place. Any place at all.

Folks talk about a town without pity but this is a city without a heart. All it has is the mouth to take you in, chew you up, taste you a little bit, and then spit you out.

People live in this city. But more of them die. Some by liquor, others by dope, hope, or bad dreams. And then all the rest by cancer or some other rotting disease. God help me I live here but I want out so bad I could taste it. I could just taste it.

This Room of Mine

Female—late 20s

I'm not sure I know how to explain this, but it's interesting and strange. . . . When you leave home, you remember things one way. When you come back, you find it's all different and changed. Now I ain't been gone that long. Just a few years. But now that I'm back I find that everything's changed. The place, the people and even this room. Everything in here is almost the way I left it, but somehow or other it just ain't the same. It's like there are ghosts standing or sitting everywhere. One in the corner, one under the bed, one by the window, another rocking in the rocking chair over there, and one lying on the floor looking up at the ceiling. But the thing is all the ghosts look like me at different ages. Me with my hair in braids, me with braces on my teeth, me with my first pair of sunglasses, me looking out the window wearing only jeans and a bra. Me, standing in front of the mirror with only a towel around me all wet and clean. All the dreams and ideals I used to have is here in the room with them, too. But now they don't belong to me anymore. They belong to them. I feel like an intruder, an outsider in this room where I was born and where I grew up. I feel like an alien who just landed from another planet. I don't belong here anymore. I never should've come back. This room is too full of ghosts and too full of memories. And the scariest part of it is all those ghosts and memories were once me.

Waiting My Turn

Female—any age

The breaking part was easy, girl. It took a long time but when it came down to the moment it was so much easier than I thought it would be. After our last little disagreement or whatever that was, he started to hesitate and stammer and I knew what was coming. He was going to tell me that he think that we should break up, and I would then say like I always did before that, just because we had one little fight that was no reason for us to bust up our relationship. We had been through this so many times that I already knew all the dialogue. So this time I thought, "Why not change things a little bit. See where it takes us." So before he could get a word out, I said, "I think we should break up. This relationship's going nowhere, so why not call it a day right now."

Girl, you shoulda seen the expression on his face. It woulda been worth at least a month's pay. "You want to what?" he asked and I said, "You heard me." And with that I got up and left him sitting there waiting for the waitress to bring the two drinks we had ordered.

Four years down the drain in one sweet, satisfying moment. Since then, he's been calling, leaving messages on my machine, and I ain't been answering. Let him sweat a little for all the times he made me sweat. I know I don't want to go back to him. And I won't. But I like it that he's begging. Damn it, I begged long enough. Now it's his turn.

Fools and Dreamers

Female—late 20s

What you or nobody seem to want to understand or appreciate is that Tupac and me is two people in love. I know that it don't sound right and maybe it don't look too good either, me being a married woman and all. But for the first time in my life I have a man who makes me feel excited and happy. This never happened to me before. So although it don't look right to other people, it feel right to me. So I got to go where my heart lead.

I know I sound like a child just born this morning talking about love as though it was something out of a book or a movie. But that's how I feel, Mama. That's how I feel in spite of the fact that you told me it wouldn't be that way. Ever since I was a child all you kept telling me was not to expect too much outta life or men. And that love was something only for fools and dreamers. And I listened, Mama. I did. But you was wrong. What you told me was right for you but wrong for me. I'm just finding that out. You married for love and that man ran away from you. I married for security and I can't stand to be in the same room with him.

I done already made one mistake; I don't plan on making another. I'm getting a divorce so Tupac and me can be together forever and ever. And the sooner everybody get used to the idea, the better off things will be for all concerned. You hearing me, Mama? If you want for you and me to be friends, you better start getting used to this situation right here and now.

A New Understanding

Female—40s

Don't think I don't know how you men talk. Boasting and bragging to all your friends in pool halls and bars. Talking about your conquests and things you made us do in those moments of passion and intimacy. Don't think I don't know because I do. And don't tell me that you're not like that. That you're different, because I know better. You're all the same. Young or old, black or white, deep down inside you're all rotten and lowdown. So don't try to tell me that you're any different.

I gave myself to you and I was sincere. I didn't ask for anything in return. I haven't been pushy or selfish. I have tried to be discreet and at the same time honest. But that isn't appreciated, is it? Instead of gratitude or appreciation all I've gotten from you is humiliation and disrespect. And it's got to stop. I'm not somebody who fell into your bed because she couldn't help herself. I'm not some lonely old woman you're doing a favor for. I might be older than you but I'm not old. I have my energy, my strength, and my resources. I'm a woman with some position in this community. People respect me and I demand the same respect from you. Just because you're young doesn't give you the right to be that way to me. Especially when you know I love you so much. So, what do you say? Let's start over again but this time with a new understanding—please?

Trust

Female—30s

You what? You've been seeing another woman. I—I can't believe that you're saying this to me . . . Another woman . . . Goddamn me . . . And all the time I thought . . . Oh God . . . Oh God. And you have the nerve to say that it's not important? You drop a casual statement that's about to pull my life apart and you say it's not important. Not to you, maybe. But it is to me. Every single detail of it is important because I want to know. I want to understand where I went wrong. Because you see, I don't believe you. I really don't goddamn believe you. I'm out there busting my back while you were in some hotel room screwing your brains out. Or was it some buddy's apartment? Tell me, I want to know. I really, really want to know.

When I think of all the opportunities I've had. And all the men that tried to proposition me. Wealthy men, handsome men. Some I was even attracted to. But I never even considered it. You want to know why? This'll hand you a laugh. Because I believed in what we had. And I also thought we were building something together. Isn't that hilarious? Isn't that the biggest joke of the year so far? Doesn't that just make you bend over and roll on the floor in hysterics? . . . Goddamn you, goddamn the day you were born. You've taken my hope, my love, and my trust and thrown them in the garbage. I hope you feel like a king. I hope you feel like a giant. I really hope you do.

The Big Mistake

Female—mid 30s

The big mistake I made was getting married. I shoulda thought twice and maybe I shoulda run the other way. But I didn't know any better and I thought I was in love. Maybe I was, too. I don't know.

He had that big car that he spray paint himself. A Buick people used to call "the Flash" on account of the fact that he used to drive it so fast. And I would sit back in it with my sunglasses on and my eyes closed feeling the speed and listening to the stereo. He was cool, I was cool. The whole world was cool in those days.

Lonny was playing baseball for the Sixty-Niners and everybody was saying that it was only a matter of time before the pro teams would be recruiting him. Every Thursday night I used to go to watch him play and cheer him on.

Now he always used to drink a little bit too much, but I didn't think it was a fault. Heck, I used to drink a little bit myself. Everybody we knew used to like to drink after the game. That was part of the ritual. Part of the routine.

When he asked me to marry him, my Daddy said, "Think about it carefully. Marriage is a big step." I did and I had some questions about Lonny, but I went and did it anyway. "Everything gon' be alright," I told myself. "I will settle down, he will settle down, and everything gon' be just fine." Well, I was wrong. I managed to settle down, but he got worse. The drinking has taken over his life and now it's taking over ours. I can't let my life go down the drain because, just because he's doing it. We have children to think about. Their futures to look after. We can't live like this so I'm going to have to go. . . . I made a mistake. A real big mistake. And now it's time to correct it.

Never Again

Female—30s

Well, I've done it. Made a clean break. It's over, done, fini. A few tears were shed, a little misery spread, but all in all I think it was the best thing for everybody. Leo and I were drifting further and further apart, and I think it's time we—well started coming back together again. After all, I did marry the man. And it wasn't so we could live together like strangers. I mean, Leo may have his faults but I think we can work them out. At least I think we should try.

And the other thing is, I'm tired. Adultery takes a lot of energy and guile. I don't want to do it anymore. I'd rather sit home at night and watch TV and not worry that every time the phone rings it's Kenny calling to tell me how much he loves me. Do you know he even sends me e-mail declaring his love? It's too much. I have to go and take it off the computer before Leo could see it. Having somebody in love with you is nice, but it can get to be too much. I never thought I'd ever say that, but it's true. That kind of love can lock you in a prison and that's the last thing I want. So I broke it off with him. He told me I was a bitch and that he never wants to see me again. I'm sorry about that but I'm glad it's over. And I'll tell you what I've learned. The next time I think about having an affair, I'll think twice, three, four, and five times. And you know what? I probably won't ever do it again.

Mr. Nice Guy

Male—mid to late 20s

A guy comes out, does some pushups and a few calisthenics, then stops and looks at the audience.

I am not a well man. In spite of what you just saw I am not a well man. Lungs *(Tapping his chest)* shot to hell. TB. Picked it up years ago but I don't know how. But it's taking me away inch by inch.

I shouldn't even be up in weather like this, with all that snow coming down and all that cold wind blowing. I should be in bed wrapped up and warm. But if she comes home and finds me in bed, there'll be another fight. She'll call me no-account and lazy. And wonder why she have to go out to work in this weather while all I do is stay home and watch TV. I tell her I'm sick and she says I'm making it up. *(He coughs a clear healthy cough.)* Does that sound like I'm making it up? I could be dead tomorrow but she don't want to recognize that. Some people, some women can be so insensitive and cruel sometimes. If I didn't love her I wouldn't put up with any of it. I would walk out of this place and that would be the end of it. But I'm not like that, so I'll stay. I'll let her hurt my feelings, let her call me names. When I think about it I know I'm too good for her, too nice to her, too. But, what the heck, that's how it is when you're truly in love.

The Optimist

Male—mid 30s

How can you miss somebody you never cared about? Somebody you thought was venial and silly and shallow and stupid and pretentious and dull and, and oh yes—humorless. That's right, "without a sense of humor." . . . How do you miss somebody like that? And more than how: *Why?* It's been plaguing me for days now. More than days, it's weeks. Weeks going into months. And more months. And it's making me crazy. Not clinically or certifiably crazy. That would be a relief. They could put me away and I would have new issues to deal with. Then perhaps I wouldn't think of her so much, or even at all. But no such luck. I'm one of the countless millions who have to carry the pain, frustration, and craziness inside while going around pretending that all the useless and senseless little routines of life are neces-sary and important. If I really had any courage I would kill myself. But I don't, so I go through the routines telling myself that there's a better day ahead, when I know damn well that there isn't. (*Holding up his glass*) To life—a comedy in one act, with a very, very bad ending.

Everybody's Baffled

Male—28

Well it was like this. We was girlfriend and boyfriend who said "I love you" to each other all the time. But when I tried to take it further, she told me, "No. We gotta wait till we're married." When I asked her why, she said, "Then it'll be right. Everybody say so." When I asked her who was everybody, she just said "Everybody." . . . We never did marry. She went her way and I went mine. She got married, had a bunch a kids and so did I. But I never stopped thinking about her. Not all the time, of course. But every now and then. . . . Every now and then I thought about her and how we wound up frustrated because she wanted to do what everybody thought was right.

It's now a buncha years later and I just got the news that she killed herself and didn't even leave a note. Not a hint, not a clue. Everybody say she always looked so happy and always so together and organized.

But something must've gone wrong, don't nobody know what. She was a good mother, they say. Her husband said he loved her and that he is baffled, too. Everybody is baffled. And everybody think it's a shame. And I think so too, because that's what she got for listening to other people.

How It Was Back Then

Those were funny times, Man. I don't mean funny—you know what I'm saying. There were civil rights confrontations erupting every day. King was preaching one thing. Malcolm was advocating something else. Folks was getting stirred up but they didn't know which way to turn.

I remember one afternoon I was visiting some friends up in Harlem and this group of guys came by. "We going to hear Malcolm speak," they told us and my buddy Archie said, "Come on, let's go." I had heard some of Malcolm's stuff on TV and I didn't want to go. I had been out late the night before and I was still tired. But clearly Archie and them others wanted to, so I went along.

The crowd was thick, and Malcolm was talking out. I don't have any real idea of what he said but I remember he talked about "house niggers" and "field niggers." Then he told the crowd, "I want you to know what I am. I'm a field nigger." The people went wild, clapping and cheering. Somebody from the crowd yelled out something, and Malcolm said, "I can't hear you brother, could you speak louder." And I guess the cat did. I can't tell you what he said, but whatever it was somebody didn't like it, 'cause the next thing I knew the man was unconscious and people was carrying him out.

"You don't put down Brother Malcolm," Archie said. "Not in this crowd." So I assumed the man said something disparaging and somebody took offense. What I couldn't figure was why he would be so stupid as to voice his opposition out loud. When a man is that stupid, he's got to pay the price. Didn't he know that?

The Last Word

Male—30s

I listen to you, Man, and sometimes I begin to think that maybe we come from two different worlds. I mean we grew up together and all, but still we so far apart in the way we think, I sometimes feel that one of us come from some place far, far away. Don't you know that the sisters hate us. We is the enemy man. Anything that ever go wrong for a black woman, the black man is to blame. Don't you know that? Don't you watch TV, read the newspapers or anything? Black men are the scum of the earth, it's as simple as that.

You tell a sister one thing, she gon' tell you it's another. You tell her right, she gon' tell you it's wrong. You tell her something is up, she gon' tell you it's down. So getting yourself upset over what Jonelle says or how the woman is acting to me is dumb. Worse than dumb, it's a waste of time. You worrying about the enemy when all the enemy is concerned about is how to see you dead or break you so bad that even your best friends wouldn't recognize you. If that's what you want, then go on. Drink up all the liquor in this place and smoke all the stuff that man in the back room selling. But don't say I didn't warn you. And when you find yourself in that deep, dark hole looking up, don't call me, cause I ain't gon be around. This is my last word to you and now I'm out of here. (*He exits*)

Dumb or Something

Male—teens

My parents make me laugh sometimes. I got into this scene a week ago where I threatened to kick Lyle Hansen across the schoolyard because he was bugging Leslie, who happens to be my girl. I mean he was calling her up all the time asking her to go out with him. Now everybody knows that she's going out with me. So him trying a thing like that is like showing no respect to me. So I talked to him and he was getting kinda rude, so I had to straighten him out. Straighten him out real fast. Action-hero style. Slam, bam, and wham!

Anyway, somehow it got to my mother who talked to me about violence and asked my father to talk to me. Only thing is my old man is in jail doing two-to-four for armed robbery. What's he going to say to me? "Don't be like me, boy?" Of course I ain't going to be like him. Who want to spend their life behind bars when everybody else is out having fun?

So come Saturday we gon' go over to see him like we always do. He gon' tell me to take care a my mother and behave myself. I'm going to say, "Yes Dad, no Dad," and act like I'm listening. And I would if he was a banker or a lawyer or a cop maybe. But I ain't listening to no jailbird. What do they think I am, dumb or something?

The Old Club

Male—50s

You young people can't see it, I know. But this place used to be hot. Used to be jumping with life and music. With moving bodies covering every inch a this floor you standing on right this minute.

She and her husband Mose used to supply the music. Every Friday and Saturday night they used to fill this place up, just to hear them play. Him on that horn and her on that piano. Wasn't nobody round these parts hotter in them days. Nobody, nobody, nobody.

She was a good-looking woman too. It's hard to recognize now I know. But she used to be. Just take my word for it. And he was, too. A handsome figure of a man standing in that spotlight with that trumpet in his hand. Women used to want to get up close and personal with all that talent and power. And many of them did, too. No-o-o, he wasn't a man to deny a pretty woman her desires. No sir.

Where did it all go wrong? Who knows? Too much success at the beginning. Too much drinking. Not enough attention paid to the business, I suppose. I don't know. But somewhere, somehow, something did go wrong. Or maybe the novelty just wore off. Who knows? But, whatever it was the people just stopped coming. And the place turned into a ghost town with only echoes and memories of the noise that used to be.

Mose, he took more to his bottle, and then to his bed. Then one day he just expired. And that was it. The trumpet sat in the corner but the sounds it made was just a memory now.

She tries to run the place, what's left of it. But it's taking its toll. I can see that. So can you. Sometimes to please herself she will sit at the piano and play. Sometimes she'll even sing. But it ain't like it was in the glory days. The voice is gone and even her piano playing ain't what it used to be. The notes sound sour where they used to be sweet. Now I think it's just a matter of time before one of them goes. She or the business.

What can I tell you. It's just sad, that's all. Just sad. But that, too, is the story of life.

What Is the Answer?

Male—late teens

So after all the kissing and touching the woman say to me, "No. I can't." So I asked her why. I mean we had got this far, why stop now? "Because I don't want to," she say to me and again I asked her why. "Because I don't feel that way about you." "Then why'd you let me get my engine all revved up?" I asked her. "I don't know. I thought that it might be enough. But it wasn't. I'm sorry."

"You sorry? How you think I feel?"

She didn't say nothing. We just sat there in the car. She on one side, me on another. A minute ago we were real close, now we're like two strangers or enemies.

"I better take you home," I said to her. "Yeah, okay," she answer back.

When we got to her place she touch my face and said, "This really got nothing to do with you. I'm just in a bad place right now. I like you a lot. You're really nice."

"Yeah, but being nice ain't getting me nowhere."

"One day it will," she said and left. This is the third girl that told me I'm nice then left me high and dry. While I look around and see bad guys making out like bandits. Is that what I have to do to get laid? Change my character and become a gangsta rapper bad guy? I mean, I don't know. But something got to be done because I can't take this kinda rejection too much longer. No sir, I absolutely can't.

Somebody Cares

Male—40s

I used to know Jamil when he wasn't the way he is now. I had this service station and he used to work for me, pumping gas, fixing cars, that kinda thing. He was good with his hands. I didn't have to teach him much. And he was a good worker. I always used to say to him, "Boy, it wouldn't surprise me any if one day you open your own service station and maybe become my biggest competitor. You got the talent and you got the brain. With a combination like that you'll go far." But he would always smile and shake his head and say, "No, Mr. Burton, this business ain't for me. I got other things I want to do with my life."

What he wanted to be was a tap dancer and he was taking lessons twice a week from an old-timer across town. He was good, too. I seen him a couple a times doing some stuff with his feet. I liked it. I liked it a lot.

Then that woman came along. They was together for a while, then she took off. Just upped one day and got in the wind. Next thing I knew, he took off, too, following her. People told him she wasn't much. She looked good, yes, but her character wasn't nothing to write home about. Still he wasn't listening. The boy was in love. Too much in love. And nothing can hurt a man worse than being too much in love.

They say he shot a man and rob three places just trying to make an impression on her. They say she's gone again. To parts unknown. Him they got locked up and say he gon' remain that way for a long, long time. Damn shame. Damn, damn shame. I liked that boy and still do. Maybe I'll write him a letter and send him some money. I just want him to know somebody in the world think about him and care. That's all. I just want him to know that.

Dear Mom

Male—late teens, early 20s

Dear Mom,

It's ridiculous for you to worry about me here in this city. I keep telling you that I'm old enough to take care of myself. And you keep refusing to believe that this is so.

New York is a city like any other place. It just got more people, that's all. The job is fine. The people treat me well. The pay ain't all that much but I'm managing. My apartment ain't big either but it's okay. I'm getting to know my way around the train and stuff. So that's making things better. I'm also starting to meet people and go out, so don't start thinking I'm lonely or anything like that. And even if I was, I'd have to deal with it, wouldn't I?

Look, I can't even think about coming home now. I just got here. I won't even be due a vacation from my job till a year from now. So don't keep asking when I'm coming home. Or telling me who missing me. I ain't coming so there ain't no point in talking about it.

Momma, believe me when I tell you that I'm fine. And that this city is where I want to be. Where my dreams and ambitions reside. Home didn't have anything for me and that's why I left. To pursue my dreams. And that's what I'm doing. Pursuing my dreams. So please, please stop worrying.

Say hello to Pops and tell him what I told you. I'm fine, and I'll always keep in touch.

> I love you both.
> Your son,
> Kyle

1½ TO 2 MINUTES

I Used to Dream

Female—late 20s, early 30s

I used to dream about living in a penthouse and now I'm living in one. I used to dream about being famous and having money. I have money and I am famous, up to a point. Every time one of my movies come out I go on TV and magazines write articles about me. Strangers walk up to me on the street and talk to me like they'd known me all my life. Some even ask for my autograph. I guess that's what being famous is. People knowing who you are, but you not knowing them.

I used to dream about all those things and one by one I got them. How? I don't exactly know. Luck? Talent? Being in the right place at the right time? Sure. But sometimes I ask myself, Why me? Why not somebody else? Not that I'm complaining. Don't get me wrong. I like where I am, but sometimes I just can't help wondering.

"Be careful what you pray for because you might get it" is a remark I heard when I was a girl. I didn't know what it meant. I mean, I understood it, but why wouldn't you want what you pray for?

Now I think I have a better idea what it means. I'm famous, I have money, I even have awards. What I don't have is somebody to hold me close.

I have guys who want to and call me up all the time. My problem is I don't know if it's me they want to hold on to or the idea of me that they see up on the screen. Or maybe it's not even that. It's my bank account that's the most attractive part of me as far as they're concerned, so I have to be careful. I've been ripped off a few times and I didn't like the experience. Still I've got to trust somebody. Got to let somebody in. The question is, Who?

(*A brief pause*) And you say you want to be famous. I'll tell you like I heard it all those years ago: Be careful what you dream for, because girl, look out, you just might get it.

An Exchange of Glances

Female—late 30s

I was so-o afraid. I didn't know how I was going to face them. I mean, here I was 37 and my marriage was falling apart. It had been a long time happening, but for the sake of the children and mostly for my parents, I pretended and pretended that this wasn't so. Then when I couldn't take it any longer I told Carl and he was surprisingly understanding. I guess he must've been feeling the same thing, too.

Now the job was to break it to my parents. We're talking here about two people who have been married for close to 50 years and to the best of my knowledge never looked at another soul with anything resembling a romantic notion. Two people who go to church every Sunday and who think that marriage is a bond for life. And people who get divorced are weak and shallow and totally without character. Two people who gave us a big wedding and over the years thought of Carl as maybe the best son-in-law ever.

I'm a grown woman and I shouldn't be concerned about this. My happiness should come first. And I haven't been happy for a long time. But I was concerned and I really didn't know how I was going to break it to them. I kept putting it off again and listening to them make plans for Carl and me and the kids. Finally one night when I couldn't take it any longer, I just said it. No preparation, no preamble. Nothing. Just one simple, declarative sentence. "Carl and I are getting a divorce." . . . First there was silence. Then an exchange of glances. Then my father finally spoke. "It's about time," he said. "We wondered when you would get around to making the decision."

"You knew?" I asked. "We sensed," he said. "You've been unhappy for a long time. We could see that, and we sort've figured out why. Whatever help you need we'll be there. Just tell us what it is."

I couldn't believe my ears. All these years I thought of them as two old-fashioned people with a narrow view of the world. Then I realized the one with the narrow view was me. I had a narrow view of my parents and now this crisis has opened my eyes. Only thing I wonder now is: What else don't I know about my parents?

Appetites and Horses

Female—30s

The biggest eater I ever knowed was a man named Duppy. His real name was Ike Wallace but everybody called him "Duppy," I don't know why. He worked for my grandfather taking care of his horses when my Gramps was still renting horses for parades and movies. There wasn't nothing about a horse that he couldn't handle, they used to say. And everybody liked him. Duppy was a big man with a big mustache and a big broad smile behind it. He had a deep, big voice, too. Duppy is what people used to call "a man's man," I guess. He had a hearty personality. He enjoyed hugging women to his chest and clapping men on their backs.

Now his wife Maya was just the opposite of him. She was small and quiet and didn't smile much. But she was a hard worker and she could really cook. That musta been the reason why Duppy married her, we girls in the yard used to say because there wasn't nothing else about her that we could see that could interest a man. Especially somebody as good-looking and full of life as Duppy.

It used to be our favorite thing, my brother, my sister, and me, to watch Maya serve up the food and watch Duppy eat. First there was the bread. He would cut a big slice, cover it with butter, and take it all down while drinking beer and telling jokes to all us kids. Then she would give him a big bowl of salad. Lettuce, cucumbers, tomatoes, pineapple chunks, and cheese. After that he was ready for his steak or side of beef that was always too big for the plate. He liked his meat rare. Cut it open and little streams of blood would pour out on the plate. Duppy wasn't a fancy man. A knife, a fork, and a thick piece of bread was all he needed to go to work on that meal. His wife, in contrast, ate like a bird. A peck here, a peck there. They were like a comic act to watch at the dinner table.

The funny thing about Duppy is that he wasn't fat. He was solid and large and very strong. But he wasn't fat. Musta been all that physical activity he had all day with the horses.

When my grandfather died, my grandmother sold the ranch and Duppy and his family went with it. He used to visit us for a while, while we was growing up. Then it dropped off and we lost contact. Neither my brother, my sister, or I know what became of him or his wife or their children. Still I remember him mostly for his appetite, and for the way he could handle horses. And I guess it was from him that I learned to love them, too.

True Love

Female—late 30s

Don't nobody I know understand anything about love. They talk about it all the time. My mother, my friends, that so-called social worker they send me, too—everybody. Everybody talk, everybody is an expert. But everybody don't know a damn thing. First off they expect love to make sense. And love don't ever make sense. If it did, the right people would always marry the right people and everything would be fine. There would be no divorce lawyers and no divorce courts. Everything would be smooth. Smooth as the ocean on a calm summer day. But love ain't like that. Love is rough and hard and mean. Love is unpredictable and nasty. And sometimes if you lucky, love is nice. Not all the time. Just a little bit here and there. But when it's nice it's so damn good that that's all you dream about through all the bad times. And all the mean times.

Everybody is down on me because I marry a man who is in prison for killing two people. They see one side of him, I see another. The man I see and love ain't no killer. That was another man who existed long ago. That man is gone and maybe even dead. The man I married is a gentle, loving person who wouldn't harm the fur on a pussycat. We met through a class at night school. I was going there because after that little problem I had with substance abuse my therapist suggested that I go after my high school diploma so's I could later go to college maybe.

Anyway, one of our assignments was to write a letter to somebody we didn't know. I found his name in a church newspaper asking people to communicate with those less fortunate than us with a word of encouragement and hope. So that's what

I did. To my surprise the man wrote back and that's how it began. Then after a while I was visiting him. And now we is husband and wife. After my pile of troubles with the law, everybody, my mother included, was saying that nobody was going to want a woman like me as a woman or a wife. And in a way, they was right. Nobody did until Terry. Now they saying I've gone crazy for doing what I've done. That I don't understand what love and marriage is about. But I think they is the ones who ain't understanding that after all these years I finally found what I been searching for all along. And what it was they was telling me I wouldn't find. True love. I found it, I got it and now it's mine all mine. And them that don't care for it? Well, too damn bad.

A Woman's Emotions

Female—mid to late 20s

I shoulda run him outta town. Shoulda thrown my shoe at him that Monday morning when he walk into my kitchen smiling and looking like there ain't nothing at all in the world wrong. Like we didn't have a history of taking and using and running away from. That man stood there talking and smiling like he was our oldest and best friend in the world, and my husband stood there looking like he is the biggest damn fool in the neighborhood. And all I wanted to scream was, "Man, don't be looking happy like you just found some long lost member of your family. Don't you know who this man is?" This is a man who smile to your face, eat up your dinner, and then when you wasn't looking started to come on to your wife. And because she was a fool, and because you wasn't doing right by her, she let him continue, and even agreed to see him in his room. And when she did, what he knew would happen did. And fool that she was, she went back for seconds and thirds and fourths and fifths until the day she said the magic word and that man went running like somebody was firing bullets at him. The magic word was love. That's all that she said. She told the man, "I love you," and it was like she had given him a needle. That man whole body froze up. And when she asked him what was wrong, all he could say was, "Nothing . . . Nothing." And the next thing she know, he was gone. No message, no note or nothing. Just gone, gone, gone. And she had to fend for herself and pull her emotions back to where they belonged. It wasn't easy and it took a long time, because fool that she was, she had really let herself fall in love with a man who didn't deserve to get the time of day from a clock. That's the kind of fool she was . . . And now three years later I had to stand there and pretend that I was glad to see him. And tonight I got to cook food and treat this man like family when all I want to do is pour something down his throat and watch him fall on the floor strangling to death.

But I'm going to try and go through with my part because I can't do anything else. And because, according to my husband, they still is best friends. I just hope and pray that I can hold it together. Because I ain't ever been the kind a woman to hide her feelings too well. Whatever I think or feel always have a way a getting out. People tell me it's a fault but that's the way I am. I can't help it. That's the way God made me. And like I said, I'm going to try. But if in the middle of the dinner I forget myself and bust that man upside his head with a saucepan or something, that's the way it is. Them's the chances you take when you mess with a woman's emotions. A woman like me anyway.

Learning to Love Jazz

Female—any age

I never used to like jazz. I don't mean that I hated it. I just never paid much attention to it, is all. It's supposed to be the real black music and all of us is supposed to like it and revel in it. But it never did nothing for me. It was just musical noise, like so many other things. I liked rock, rhythm n' blues, and Gospel. But jazz, be-bop, fusion, and progressive was something I never could get into.

Then Brandon changed it for me. He was this white guy I kinda brought into my apartment because he looked so pitiful and lost. And so skinny he looked like he hadn't eaten in a month. And he was pitiful and lost, but in a gentle kind of way.

We met because he came to my shop and asked if I had any work he could do to make some money. I looked at this fellow, dirty and raggedy but good-looking and indigent, and I decided to help him right then and there. There was work in the store needing to be done. Then there was work at my apartment, too. Shelves that was broken, closets that needed to be cleared out, walls that could use some paint. He did it all and more. And I kept asking him to come back. Even after most of the work was done I kept finding reasons for him to come back the next day and the day after that. Well, one thing led to another—I don't want to go into it—but we got close. Romantic, intimate . . . you know what I mean. There was something about him that was like a saint or an angel . . . or maybe a child. He didn't talk loud, was always grateful for what he got, and never asked for anything but was always grateful for what he got. I knew it wouldn't last. Couldn't last. It was too good and too special. So I didn't expect anything from day one. But it lasted longer than I expected. Three weeks to be exact. Then one day he didn't say anything. He just left. I wasn't upset. I knew it would come to that and it did. He wasn't from my world. He was just passing through. But what I remember most about him was his love of jazz. It was the only possession he carried around with him. A bunch of CDs in a backpack. And everything he did, from work to making love, he wanted to have that music playing in the background. Until I heard and felt it in a romantic context I never had any idea how warm and subtle and sensual it was. Now it's the only music I listen to all the time.

Now I have over 100 CDs and my library grows bigger every week. My new boyfriend asked how I got into this jazz thing and I told him that I've been listening to it ever since I was a child. . . . A woman got to have some secrets. And this one is mine.

Sometimes I think that the only reason Brandon drifted into my life was to teach me how to appreciate and love jazz. And for that I'll be ever grateful to you, Brandon, wherever you are.

Parts Unknown

Female—30s

You got to keep that door shut and you always got to check who you letting in or even talking to on the phone. I know that I sound like I'm paranoid but that ain't the case. I like you and I want you to stay. That's why I'm telling you this stuff.

It's about my boy, Lamarr. I'm his mother but I ain't supposed to have him. When his father and I divorce, he got a high-price lawyer. And between him and that lawyer they got the judge to give him full custody of our child. My child. The one that I conceive and carried inside me for nine months. Said that because of my, well, "problem," that I was an unfit mother. I could visit him on weekends and stuff but he couldn't live with me. This is the same man who when the child was born didn't want to have anything to do with me or it. Who even went so far as to suggest that the child wasn't his, until his mother had to step in and say to him, "Do right by that girl, boy!" And by that she meant "Acknowledge paternity of that child and pay child support. But don't marry her." And that's what he did. Then he had a change in life and got into politics. Suddenly him and his righteous wife wanted everything done right. And all their children living in one household. Including mine. So he went out and got this big-shot lawyer. Then they got the judge to pass down the verdict.

I didn't say nothing because I knowed that if I said anything, he and his sharp-shooting lawyer would see to it that I got no visiting rights whatsoever. So for damn near seven months I did like I was supposed to do. Take him out for half a day, play with him in the park, and bring him back when they told me. It broke my heart but I did like I was told to. Then one Saturday I took him and we didn't come back. We got on a plane and left for parts unknown. It wasn't planned or premeditated or nothing like that. I got the idea that morning while watching a TV program about the Witness Protection Program the Feds set up for criminals who squeal. Then and there I decided to set up my own protection program and that was it. This here is "parts unknown," but you never can tell. His father got money and power and if I know that man like I think I do, he ain't gon' stop till he has detectives or the police knocking on that door.

My child is mine and I don't plan on giving him up. But I don't plan on getting caught either. Not if I can help it. So you gon' move in and I'm glad you moving in, but you got to be careful. That's all I'm telling you. We got to be real, real careful about who we talk to and who we let in.

With No Clothes On

Female—mid 20s

See, I was standing there naked, because that's what you do when they paying to model in a Live Figure art class. I mean it was something you don't have to know anything about it. You just stand there naked, pose like they tell you, and the teacher tell them what to draw or paint. Every fifteen minutes they give you a break. So you put on a robe and relax or drink some water or whatever else you like. It's an easy way to make some money and the hours ain't too long. When I first came to this city, I did all kinds a jobs. Waiting tables mostly. People told me I had a cute body and guys were hitting on me all the time. Some older men even offered to support me and stuff like that. Of course I didn't pay them no mind. I was interested in studying and becoming an actress. And I still am. But my work hours were long and I needed more time for myself. That's when I heard about this "live modeling" thing. I saw an ad for it in the newspaper so I went in and interviewed. Now I'm doing it and I like it. I like it a lot but it has its downs. It has its ups, but it definitely has its downs.

Now the good thing about it is that although you naked and all, don't nobody bug you about—well, you know what. In the restaurants with all my clothes on they did. But here with no clothes on, they don't. Sometimes you kinda wish somebody might say something because there are some cute guys in the class. And I wouldn't mind getting to know one or two of them. But like I said, everybody acts respectable and decent. Soon as class is over they pack their stuff up and leave. And that's how it goes.

Now there was this one guy from the class I kinda got to know for a minute. We used to talk during the breaks sometimes. Then we met at this party one night and he began to talk to me like he was interested in us hanging out together. Or maybe going out on a date. When I saw that he didn't recognize me, I told him who I was. He said, "Oh yes, I thought there was something familiar about you," and then he was gone. Some weeks later I ran into him on the street and asked him why he never called me like he said he would. He said that he already knew too much about me and that I had no mystery for him. And I thought, What a jerk and what a shit he is. But still he was kinda cute. . . . Of course he knows nothing about me except the way I look with no clothes on. Still he think he knows all there is to know. But that's what I mean when I say this job has its ups and downs.

The Quick Thinker

Male—30s

I look at myself in the mirror and sweat is pouring off me. I feel my chest and my heart is like a fist pounding in there. But I got to say I'm all right. Scared yes, panicked and anxious, yes. But I'm all right. Only thing is I need a drink to calm me down. A big one, too. Boy, that was close. Too close. I don't ever want to be in a situation like that again. No sir. Never, never again. I don't exactly know how I got out of it, but God was good. That's all I got to say: God was very good to me on this day.

I mean . . . I mean, there I am laid up and sleeping in the woman's bed, and maybe I was even smiling, I don't know, when I feel this hand shake me and shake me and shake me again hard. When I open my eyes it's Charleyne's boyfriend Roscoe standing there, bigger n' life, looking down at me, asking, "Where's Charleyne? And what you doing here in her bed?" I mean it shoulda been obvious since I was lying there with no clothes on. And I got to tell you, for a split second my whole life flash in front of me and I could see death grinning at me saying, "I got you now, don't I? Because this man gon' kill you sure as spring follow winter." So I had to so some fast thinking. I mean real, real fast. Now the man asked a question so I figured that I better say something fast, something quick to distract his mind from what he was seeing. So I say, "Hey man, what time is it?" When he look at his watch, I jump outta the bed and said, "Damn, I'm going to be late. That man gon' fire my ass if I don't hurry! This the third time this week and that man don't tolerate lateness. He gon' fire my ass if I don't hurry up. And God knows I can't afford to lose this job. No sir, that's one thing

I sure can't afford." And I kept up the conversation talking 'bout my job and stuff while I got into my clothes and made for the door. I didn't let him get a word in edgewise. I was talking out of speed and out of nervousness, too. I just kept on talking till I hit the door, was down the stairs, and on the street. Then I said to myself, Feet, do your stuff, and I double-timed it back here and locked the door. Now Charleyne and I ain't no couple or nothing like that. This was just a one-night thing that come together because we was working late. I made the suggestion; she said yes. And the next thing I know we was doing the nasty. . . . I don't know why she didn't wake me up when she left or maybe she did but I fell back to sleep. But man I coulda been in big trouble if I didn't think fast. Real fast.

Man, I can still see those eyes and that mean expression he had when he woke me up. I don't think I'll ever forget it till the day I die. Now the question I have to ask myself is: Was the night with Charleyne worth it? Seeing that it was just last night, I got to say, "Oh yeah."

No Reason for Tears

Male—30s

Oh yeah, I went to the funeral and took a good look at her lying there. A good-looking young woman with everything to live for, lying there in the coffin dead. People crying and saying prayers. Others bringing flowers and singing hymns. The minister shaking everybody's hand. A woman, young, healthy, lying there dead. Dead by her own hand. Why? Because she was broken-hearted they say. The woman was married to my friend, Bernie, but in love with some rapper with a name nobody can pronounce. The boy wasn't even famous or well known or nothing like that. Just a local boy trying to make a score in the area. She was carrying on with that boy and some of us knew it. But didn't none of us say anything. Wasn't any of our business. Woman want to lay up with a rapper, what's there to say? To tell you the truth, I had tried to get a little something off of her myself. I mean since she was giving some of it away, why not to me? Me being a friend of the family and all. I mean, why go to strangers when you could give it all to friends? But the woman tell me no. More than no, she wouldn't hear of it. Act like I insult her or something. So I told her I was sorry. I didn't mean to offend the woman or nothing. I was just asking, that's all. No harm in that as far as I could see.

Anyway, when she and this rapper broke up, I guess she couldn't take it. The woman flipped out. Wrote a note, then took a heavy dose of some kind of poison. Doctors couldn't do nothing. She was already dead when they arrived.

Her husband was upset, Mother upset. Hell even the damn rapper was upset. Didn't nobody know that Bea was capable of doing this kind of thing. Everybody called it a tragedy. To tell the God's truth, I was upset, too. I won't lie. I looked at her lying there thinking what a waste the whole thing was. I mean I look at them nice legs and that full round chest and that pretty, pretty face and I think "Damn—since she didn't care that much about herself, why didn't she let me get a little? Since it wasn't going to mean anything anyway, why be so damn stingy?" It wouldn'ta done her any harm and woulda done me a whole lotta good. A whole lot. . . . People want to think of her as sensitive and tragic but I think of her as selfish. And that's the reason, I'm telling you, why you won't see any tears in my eyes. No sir, no tears at all.

Insomnia

Male—early 40s

It was a mistake. A stupid mistake, I admit it. The girl was too young. I shouldn't've gotten involved. I'm a grown man and I knew better. A lot better. And it's not like I needed a woman. I coulda had several. Sensible, intelligent, mature women who were interested, and who knew how to appreciate a man like me. And they weren't secret about it either. Several of them made that abundantly clear to me. But I was stupid. What else can I tell you? I was an idiot. She was young, good to look at, and full of life. And that's what won me over. Her vitality and high spirits. She had the ability to make me laugh. So I went and got myself involved. I wasn't only happy to be involved with a woman nearly twenty years younger than myself, I went and married her, too. Many years ago my uncle Leo told me something that I forgot but I'm remembering now. He said to me one day, and I don't remember why he said it, he said to me: "Boy, don't ever marry somebody too young for you. And if you make the mistake and do, be prepared to endure a lot of pain." . . . I was young at the time so of course I didn't listen.

My problem is that I didn't know when I had it good. Before we got married I was living like a king. Sleep when I like, get up when I like, go out when I like. See who I like. Nobody to bug me or question me about it. Not that I ever was wild in my ways. But if I wanted to, I coulda been. No questions asked, no answers to be given.

But now look at me. I'm the one that's staying up late, looking at the clock, wondering where the hell she could be and who she is with. It's one o'clock in the morning and here I am looking at TV but listening for the key to click in the door. She tells me she only goes out with those boys to laugh it up and dance. Nothing more. Just for a little excitement. I guess I'm supposed to believe that. Well maybe it's true. But then again maybe it ain't. AND THAT'S WHAT MAKES ME CRAZY. I DON'T KNOW IF SHE'S LYING OR TELLING THE TRUTH.

So, look at me, staying up nights, walking the floor. Drinking!

When I got married, everybody envied me. But if my worst enemy could see me now they would be laughing. Laughing their heads off.

Why'd I go and do it? I don't know. I thought I'd found a prize. But this prize is turning into a nightmare. . . . I could walk out, of course. Ain't nothing stopping me from doing that. But I can't. And that's what the hell of it is. I can't. I'm still too much in love. So here I am in the situation that I'm in.

What I should do now is go to sleep. Take a pill and go to sleep. But I can't. I gotta be up, want to be up so I can see her and talk to her when she comes in. It'll be more lies, of course. And more attitude, too. But I can't help myself. And that's the long and the short and the tall of it. I just can't help myself.

Show Me Your Bills

Male—any age

Hey look at it, another nice day out there. And all them stretch limousines got their windows rolled down. That's what I got to get me one a these days. One of them stretch babies. Of course, those things cost bucks. Big bucks. People who own them in one of three kinds of game. Rock n' roll music, big business, or drugs.

Now I ain't a bad singer. But I didn't start young enough. See, to be in show business, you got to start when you nine. And your mommy and daddy got to be in it before you. Else you got to have some kind of handicap. A gimmick. You know—something to sell. Cause being in show business or big business is kinda like pimping. If you don't know which ass to kiss and which one to cut, you ain't gon' get nowhere. So I leave it alone since I always have trouble with c-ees and k-ays anyway.

Now the drug scene is a trip that will keep you on the run. Whether you pushing, or using. Or doing both at the same time. Always somebody behind your ass chasing it. Either a cop or a hit man. Or some damn mother with an ax shouting, "You killed my child! You killed my child!" And since I don't like having to look over my shoulder all the time in the first place, I let that scene lay.

S-o-o-o—it come round to me, standing here on a nice day, watching the world go by. And dreaming what might be. It ain't easy in America to be black, broke, and unemployed—all at the same time. Matter of fact, it hard. Sonofabitchin' hard. But I'm going to survive. I'm going to make my score. Don't you worry your head about that. No sir. I'm going to win. That's what this country and this city is about, ain't it? Winning and smiling for all the world to see. Winning. Winning, not losing.

So, now I'm going to pass round the hat. If you like what I'm saying—drop a little something in the hat. Something green, just to show your appreciation. And if you don't like what I say, stick around. There's more to come. Nobody goes away empty. Everybody gon' be satisfied. That's a promise from the soul.

Now let's see how great this country really is. Show me your bills baby. Show me your bills.

Paying the Price

Male—20s

She and I met in a restaurant. You won't believe this, but I went over to her and told her she looked like somebody I knew. Corny, right? But it was true, she did look like somebody I knew.

Anyway, after I said, "Excuse me" and all that other stuff, she told me who she was, and I told her that I was sorry for bothering her. Then she said it wasn't any bother and I said something else and—one thing led to another. Then she asked me to sit down and we spoke to each other some more.

When I asked if she'd go out with me, she said she had a date for that night. So I said, "What about tomorrow night?" And she said, "Okay."

We met and it worked out. Worked out more than I expected because, well—I wasn't expecting anything.

I told her not to get hung up on me. And she made me promise the same thing. This was only going to be a summer fling. Something to pass the idle days of summer. Come September, she would be leaving and that was just fine with me. My life was complicated enough, I didn't need to add to it.

Summer went by and the end came soon. Much too soon. She changed her mind and wanted me to stay. And I thought about it. I really did. But instead I promised that I would write and visit her. I wanted to put some time and space between us, just to make her reach a little. Just to make her appreciate me some more. It was kind of a little game I was playing, like I said, just to make her reach a little. That never happened. Later on I wrote but she never answered. She found somebody else and I became a memory, I suppose.

It was all for the best, I guess. But if it was, why is it that I think of her and wonder and wish? And ask myself, Why didn't I have the courage to face up to my feelings? And why didn't I say: I love you, please stay with me? Why did I have to play that game? And now I guess I'm paying the price.

The False Image

Male—30s

Want to hear what happened to me? A few nights ago I got home late. Like two, three o'clock in the morning. I ain't exactly sure. Put my key in the door kinda quiet not to wake up my old lady. Man, I wasn't in the room proper when that woman jump at me shouting and trying to punch me in my face. "Where was you!" she calling out. "What dirty black bitch has you been laying up with?" and noise like that. I didn't know what she was talking about. That woman is always imagining things. Always making noise. Always imagining that I been out and around laying up with some damn woman or the other. The truth is, I was out with the boys drinking, talking, and doing a little gambling. Nothing serious, just a dice game to occupy the time. I wasn't with no woman, but I didn't tell her that. Woman want to believe I'm some kind of a stud, let her believe it. She want to believe I'm some kind of coxman. Hell, I don't mind the image. I don't mind the image at all. So when she shout and ask where the hell was I, I shout back to her, "None a your goddamn business! Woman! I go where I like and lay up with who I please." And man, that really made her go wild. The woman start kicking and punching at me. I was amazed. This skinny, narrow woman was trying to knock me out with her fists. Trying so hard that I had to grab her and wrestle her down to the floor. Then I kiss her and calm her and tell her to settle herself down. Next thing I know we had our clothes off and was doing it right there.

When it was over she ask me if I ever do it like that with them other bitches that I see. I told her, "No, Honey, only with you. You is the only one who can get me excited in this kind of way." Know what she did? She smiled and said, "Good. I'm glad. Because if I thought you did, I would kill you and that's a fact." And I thought to myself, This woman is crazy. I'm married to a crazy woman. But you know what? I love her, and that's a fact.

Quoting Shakespeare

Male—19

My teacher told me if I want to be an actor, I got to learn to do Shakespeare. I asked her why. What does Shakespeare have to do with black life or the world that I come from? She said to me, it's not about the world that you come from but about the world you trying to get into . . . "The white world," I said to her. "Yes," she said to me. "That world for better or worse uses Shakespeare as the yardstick and the measure. And if you don't measure up, they won't let you in." . . . What she said made sense so I went out and bought a book and studied Shakespeare. And now I can quote him like other people know the words to their favorite rap song:

"The sense of death is most in apprehension; and the poor beetle, that we tread upon, in corporal sufferance feels a pang as great as when a giant dies." *Measure for Measure,* act 3, scene 2

"The undiscovered country from whose bourn no traveller returns, puzzles the will, and makes us rather bear those ills we have than fly to others that we know not of?" *Hamlet,* act 3, scene 1

"There's no bottom, none, in my voluptuousness: your wives, your daughters, your matrons and your maids, could not fill up the cistern of my lust." *Macbeth,* act 4, scene 3

"Even as one heat another heat expels, or as on nail by strength drives out another, so the remembrance of my former love is by a newer object quite forgotten." *Two Gentlemen of Verona,* act 2, scene 4

"Care keeps his watch in every old man's eye.
And where care lodges, sleep will never die.

But where unbruised youth with unstuff'd brain
Doth couch his limbs, there golden sleep doth reign."
Romeo and Juliet, act 2, scene 3

There you see. You thought I was lying, didn't you? But I can quote and do Shakespeare for maybe an hour straight. . . . My only problem is, I don't understand any of it. Not a word.

Derelict Ravings

Male—late teens, early 20s

I saw a bum on the street today calling out to everybody, "Hey! Hey! You all want to hear something. You all want to hear something wonderful? . . . I ain't been laid in over 8 years. Eight years and more. And I'll tell you something more. I don't care. No, I don't give a damn. Oh yeah, I used to care. I used to care about it a whole lot, but I don't any more. Nope, it don't bother me at all. Womens had their ways with me and I had my ways with them. Lots a them. Some gave me a lotta grief, and I put even more through hell. In them days, I had ambition and money. And that's what I thought the world was all about. Ambition and money and women and getting laid. Now I know different. Now that all that is gone, I see the world in a different light. A better light."

I stopped and stood and listened to this man as he kept on shouting to the world, "Getting laid, what's the big deal? Will somebody instruct me about this. What is the big Goddamn deal? You do it, you get some pleasure, you get tired, and then you go to sleep. When you wake up the world is still the same. Only thing is, the woman gone and she took your money with her. So you go after another one and the same thing happen all over again. It go on like that and one day you standing on a street corner free at last. Thank God I'm free at last."

I was standing there listening but nobody was stopping. Everybody was in a hurry. Everybody was too busy, including me.

So I went back to my little room, pulled down the shades, and hit the sack. That's what you do in a bright city. You pull down the shades to keep out the glare, and sleep by day so's you can prowl the street by night. And that bum on the street—what was it he said again? Damn, I don't remember. I wish I could, but I don't. Well, he's a derelict anyway, and who even cares what a man like that has to say.

Bad Medicine and Prayers

Male—40s

Oh man, the woman was banged up, beat up, and messed up.
The insurance people couldn't do nothing with the car so they
just junked it. Everybody was certain she would die from an
accident like that. But she fooled them and held on. Fooled
them and survived. Some people is real hard to kill. And Sara
must be one of them. So for weeks they had her in the hospital
feeding her through a straw with all kinds a people kneeling
round her saying prayers and singing. Oh man, that stuff will
mess you up worse than any car accident can. So when she start
getting better I told Phil to get his sister outta there. "Man, if
you got any interest in your sister's welfare, bring the woman
home. Get her away from that hospital as quick as possible.
They giving her bad medicine and prayers. I don't know of any
two things that will destroy a human faster." Of course he
wasn't listening. He told me those people were good Brothers
and Sisters looking out for his sister's welfare. Well, I can't tell a
man how to be with his family, so I just kept my mouth shut
after that.

But I told him what I said because I was speaking from
experience. I had a aunt who went into that same hospital for a
gall bladder operation. And just like Sara, she had them people
singing and praying all over her. Next thing I know, the woman
was dead. When I ask them "How come?" they told me she had
an advanced case of "intestinal cancer." Now I know that was a
damn lie. They was covering up their mistake. And I might've
made some legal noise about it, but I couldn't prove nothing. I
just had my suspicions, that's all. Plus, when she died she left

me a little piece of property and some money in the bank. So in a way, their mistake was my gain.

Still, I told Phil to get his sister outta there. After all, home is where the heart is, right? And you better believe me when I tell you, ain't nothing worse in this world than bad medicine and prayers. It's a lethal combination that'll kill you every time.

Hypocrisy

Male—mid to late 20s

That guy was fooling with me all night. Fool with me so much the referee had to take points from him. Two points in the third round, one in the fifth. If he had taken any more the man woulda been D–Qed and I woulda won the fight anyway. But I didn't want to win on any disqualification. I wanted to knock him out. I wanted to make that sucker pay for all them bad things he was doing to me in the ring. All them fouls. All that clowning around he was doing to try and make me look bad.

My corner kept saying to me, "Settle down, stay calm, stay focused. Winning is all that's important right now. Don't let him get you off your game." But it's hard to stay calm when you know a man is trying to damage you in there. And he was talking up a lot of stuff, too. Calling me a "pussy" and a "bitch" and stuff like that.

I wanted to knock him out so bad I could taste it. Could taste it like a nice piece of chicken cooked up good. He could box but he had a weakness. He kept his left low and he was a head hunter. All I had to do was get close, move to his right a little bit, offer him my head, and when he went for it, ground myself good and nail him with the upper cut. Nail him so hard that his jaw would go through the ceiling and he would think twice the next time he start mouthing off to somebody in the ring. So I waited my turn and in the tenth round I got my shot. A clear right hand following a feint with the jab. He went for it and I clocked him. I knew he would go because I could feel the power come from all the way in the back of my heel. He hit the canvas and the referee knew he didn't have to count. So he just waved me off. It was all over. I had won like I wanted. Big time. I had knocked that big-mouth sucker out.

Only problem is now he is in a coma. He ain't dead but he won't be much good to himself either. They want me to go visit him. Want me to say I'm sorry. Want me to say it to the press and on TV, too. My problem is, I ain't sorry. He was trying to hurt me, I just happen to hurt him first. That's the name of the game in boxing. Do it to him before he does it to you. He was a mean bastard and he got what he deserve.

But now I got to go and pretend like I'm sorry. I got to visit him in the hospital and act real sad like some member of my family died or something. I got in this profession and I thought you just got to be a boxer. Now I'm finding out you got to be an actor, too.

2½ TO 3 MINUTES

Freedom to Love

Female—19

We been knowing each other since I was a child. My parents used to take us to his house on birthdays and holidays and all kinds a other times. They was real good friends. His wife was like an aunt to me. And he was always nice to me, too. He was funny and liked to joke a lot. But he was smart. Very smart. My father used to say that he joke like that to cover up how smart he is, because people don't like it when somebody is too smart.

I musta been about sixteen when I first begin to realize that I was in love with him. Yes I was in love with this man who was one year younger than my father. And whose wife was like a second mother to me.

I told myself that what I was feeling just wasn't so. That it was just foolishness. I went out with a bunch of other boys. I even got real involved with one hoping that I could forget about Ozzie. I even tried staying away from his house and stuff, but we would run into each other at the supermarket and drug store. It was like the devil or somebody was trying to bring us together.

Now I didn't know how he felt. All I knowed is how I was feeling inside. I was wanting him to hold me, put his mouth on mine, and put his tongue against my tongue. I was eighteen by this time and everything inside me was screaming for something more than just holding hands and grabbing at each other in the back seat of a car. I was a woman and I wanted to feel like a woman. But I wanted to get all those feelings from this man.

Now like I said, I didn't know how he felt. But a person can tell when there's something there. It's just a feeling you get when that other person is in the room. And sometimes you have to take a chance on that feeling. So one day we were just talking and I said it out loud, "I love you." Wasn't nobody there but me and him, but he looked around anyway to see if anybody was watching or listening. "You don't know what you're saying," he said to me.

"Yes I do. I'm a woman and I know what I feel."

He kept trying to talk me out of it. But I told him the truth. And that was the fact that I thought about him, dreamed about him, and even pretended I was with him when I was with other boys letting them try their clumsy mess on me. I told him I wanted to be with him, not just in a dream but in the flesh. And I told him I knew he was lying when he said that he didn't want me, too. I could sense it and I knew it. The vibes coming from him was too strong for them to be anything else. I told him if he wanted to he could continue lying to himself and to me. But I wasn't going to any longer. I was going to admit how I feel and shout it out to the world if I have to. . . . Then finally, finally he admitted that he was feeling the same thing. Feeling the same feelings, thinking the same thoughts.

Two nights later we were in a motel room and it was everything I dreamed it would be and more.

"We're playing a dangerous game," he said to me. And I told him, "I know." "We have to keep this relationship secret, because even when you put the best light on it, it represents betrayal of people we love and are close to."

I knew all that but I didn't care. I didn't want to care. I just wanted to be with him more and more.

A year and a half passed by and I couldn't hold it in anymore. I had to tell somebody how I was feeling. So I told my girlfriend, Kima. She promised not to tell anybody else. But of course she did. And word got back to my parents, to his wife, and then to everybody else. His wife says she wants to see me. And in spite of what I've said my father blames it all on him.

Said the next time they meet he's going to put a bullet through his heart.

Now we don't see each other any more and Ozzie's life might even be in danger. Why? Just because I loved him and he loved me.

Attaching the Blame

Female—40s

I know the temptation in situations like this is always to blame the mother. Your son commits a crime, so naturally the parent is to blame. I know people who are doing that right now. And I suspect that my own mother is secretly pointing her finger at me as well. I can't say that I'm surprised or that I even blame them. I used to feel that way myself. About other people and their children. They do something bad it was because the child wasn't brought up right. The parents wasn't paying enough attention, and stuff like that. Now the shoe is on the other foot. Wendell is my son. I did bring him up. Where would he get those various qualities, if not from me? His father wasn't around, so he can't be blamed. Me, myself, and I. That's who was in the driver's seat. And that's who has to take the blame, if any blame is to be assigned. But I don't believe that any more. Dr. Thompson's convinced me that it doesn't have to be that way.

"Attaching blame," he said, "is society's way of explaining and accounting for behavioral patterns and deeds that are in themselves inexplicable. Things don't need a reason," he said to me over and over again. "Oftentimes, they just are phenomenons of nature, or life, just as much as hurricanes, earthquakes, or squalls might be." . . . Dr. Thompson is right. I believe that to be true, so now I don't concern myself about it anymore. Things happen because they have to happen. And there's nothing anybody can do about it. It's as simple as that. No more, no less.

But I wasn't always like this. There were nights, sometimes weeks and months on end when I would stay up wondering if I was at fault for what he did. Wondering if I drove him to it in any way. When he was drinking or taking stuff, when he stole things, ran with the wrong crowd, or broke into people's houses. Or that time when he and those other boys supposedly raped that girl and left her alone and naked in that motel room. That wasn't something I could imagine my son doing. I mean, I knew he wasn't perfect and that he could be really wild. But still it wasn't something I believed he was capable of. Then when I listened to all the reports and all the evidence the detectives and the cops were showing me, I began to believe it was true. When I heard the girl's story, then I was sure he was guilty, even though he was insisting loudly that the whole thing was a lie. That the girl had made it up. Then when she retracted her story and admitted she had made it all up, I thought to myself, See, you never gave him the benefit of the doubt. You did like everybody else and rushed in to judge him as guilty even though he told you he was innocent. You chose to believe all those strangers over your own son.

Now as I said before, Wendell isn't perfect. I know that. I know that better than anyone. But he didn't kill those two people either. My boy ain't like that. My boy ain't no killer. I don't care what the evidence says. I don't care how many eye-witnesses they got. My son says that he is innocent and I believe him. So I'm going to say this and I'm going to say it loud: HE IS NOT A MONSTER EITHER. THAT'S WHAT THEY'RE TRYING TO CHARACTERIZE HIM AS IN COURT! A MONSTER! HE IS NOT THAT! HE IS NOT THAT AT ALL. . . . And I should know. After all, I am his mother.

Hooked on a Feeling

Female—early 20s

Is this the way it supposed to be when a person is in love? I mean I didn't feel this way about any of my boyfriends before. Even with Deke. All the girls said he was a hot number and that I was lucky to be going out with him. To me he was all right. More'n all right. But there wasn't any kind a craziness. Any kinda, I don't know—excitement. I wasn't jumping outta my skin or anything like that. We went out together and we had fun, but that was it. Fun. No big thing. Then after a while he drifted away and so did I.

But with Kwami it's all different. It's—well, sexy and dangerous and sinful and violent and, er—well—full. I feel full and satisfied and uncertain all the time. I feel like somebody living out on a ledge. I can't look down because the height will scare me. And every step I take can send me falling over a cliff. But still I can't leave. But still I don't want to leave.

He say he's in love with me and I guess I believe him. I mean why else would he be with me. He could be with any woman he want to but he pick me. So I got to feel that when he say he love me he's telling the truth. Why would somebody lie about a thing like that anyway?

I used to say that I didn't want to get married. At least not while I was still young. That I was going to have a professional career, travel around the world, meet all kinds a people, and then after all that, maybe settle down. Now those things seem like just a buncha childish dreams. I want to settle down, I want to be married. And I want to have babies. Kwami's babies. Little cute black things calling me "Mama," calling him "Papa." That's what I want for myself and that's what I want for him. My problem is I don't know if he want that. And I don't know how to ask him. Because if he don't, just my asking the question might scare him away. And, oh Lord, I don't know what I would do if he left. I think I would embarrass myself and follow him wherever he went begging him to get back with me.

People talk about pride but I don't care nothing 'bout that. Pride don't hold my hand on the street or lay down next to me in bed at night. Pride don't touch me all over and make my whole body tingle and heat up with all kinds a feelings. Pride don't make me feel all warm and cuddly when I'm falling asleep, so I don't want to hear nothing about it. Kwami is the one. And Kwami you always be the one.

Now if you had told me a year ago that I would be the kind of person to feel that way about a man, I woulda called you all kinds a fool and told you to get outta my face. Now I's the one being the fool and I don't care who know it. I just know what I feel. And oh Lord, I don't want to feel any other way again ever, ever, ever.

Looking Up at Clouds

Female—20s

Sometimes I stand here looking up at the clouds and that's all I can see—clouds. No past, no present, no future. Just clouds.

How did I get into this mess? I had a future all planned out for myself. It wasn't anything special or extra. It was ordinary like everybody else. A job, some good times, vacations, meet a nice guy, get married, have some kids, and spend Christmas with family and things like that.

When you look past the clouds, you see the sky. When I was a child they used to tell me that God live up there. God with the angels and all the people who led a good life was up there flying around, talking and greeting each other. Now they telling us that what is up there is planets and stars and black holes and meteors. And when I ask people where God lives, they tell me up there, too, but in another place.

He said it would be just this one time and then we would be free to do what we want, go where we want. Sometimes at nights for days on end we would lie on the floor of his little apartment and look at travel folders of all the places we might go after it was over.

And we wasn't the only ones. Lori and Jami had plans, too. And I remember me saying, "Why this? Why we got to go in there and rob this old man in his Bodega?" And Zab saying, "Because he been robbing the people in this neighborhood ever since I was a child. Now it's time for some payback." And Jami then saying, "Plus, whatever we take off him today, he gon' make back tomorrow anyhow. So it ain't no big thing." And I thought, "Yeah, he got a point. A big point."

I went in first and Jami came in after. I asked the old man for some cigarettes and while he was getting them, Zab pulled out his piece. Lori locked the door and turn the sign around so it said closed. Jami jump back behind the counter and grab the money from the register. "Turn out the lights," Zab said, so I did. Just as that happened and we was making it to the door, I heard the first bullet fire and I heard Jami cry out, "Oh God." Then Zab fire and the old man fired again and glass broke and the alarm went off. I don't know what made me do it but I ran to the back and found a way out through a bathroom window. Then I walked down the street and didn't look back until I was blocks and blocks away.

The radio said everybody is dead. Zab, Jami, Lori, and the old man. It didn't say anything about a fourth person being there. But everybody know that me and Zab was close. So I got to figure out what to say or leave town before some damn body say they seen us together going into the store. Only thing is I can't because I ain't got any money. Besides which even if I did, where would I go? All the plans we made was for me and Zab. Now it's just me alone.

Didn't nobody plan for the old man to have a gun. Or for him to use it like he did. Now four people is dead and I'm standing here looking up at the clouds. I would do something else if I could, but I can't think of anything.

Dangerous Weather Conditions

Female—mid 30s

Did you hear the weather report? It say that a record-breaking cold is enveloping the upstate region and all along the East Coast. Record amounts of snow is going to fall and the temperature is going to drop into the single digits. Power shortages and blackouts have already been reported. The airport is closed and so is the train station. They expect this to be one of the worst winter storms to hit this area in the last ten years. Dangerous conditions, they say, exist everywhere. And I know that it's true. Look at you and me. We're here and there's nobody else. Just a lot of empty rooms, a fireplace and us.

I wrote to you and wrote to you but you never answered back. I was even tempted to drive into the city and just show up at your door. What would you have done if I had? Don't answer. I don't care. That's all in the past and I believe in living in the present. Only in the present. The here and now. And what's here and what's now is you and me. Nobody else, just you and me. And if you're afraid to say it, I'm not. I love you. I love you in all the ways a woman can love a man. And I want you in all those ways, too. I want you so much and I want you so bad that it's all I can think about most of the time. Even when I'm lying in bed with him pretending that I'm enjoying what we're doing when we make love. It's always you and it always has been you.

He's your brother and I married him. I did it out of spite. I did it because I was mad and I wanted to hurt you. Instead I hurt myself and I'm hurting him.

You're staying away from me because you think it's the faithful thing to do. The loyal thing, the brotherly thing. And I keep asking myself, When did you ever get so virtuous? I remember a time right after I got married that you came and made me betray any idea I had about being faithful right there in that guest bedroom of ours. You never said much. Never even said you love me. But action always speaks a lot louder than words.

I didn't ask you to come here. I didn't ask for this bad weather to come in on us. I didn't ask Len to be on the other side of the country either. It all just fell out that way and I don't intend to fight it. No, I'm not going to fight it at all. Instead I'm going to surrender and embrace it. Hold it close to me. Wrap my legs around it and let it feel the warmth of who I am and who you are, while the weather outside continues to blow and freeze everything. I have fires in me that are raging to burn. And I don't intend on holding them in anymore. You can resist it, you can fight it, but I'm going to win because you want me, like I want you. I can see it in your eyes. I can see it in other places, too.

"A dense coastal fog has moved inland and the cold weather continues to produce record low temperatures. According to our satellite readings, this cold snap will be with us for several more days, so caution is being advised in all outdoor activities. Indoors, dangerous conditions exist as well. But what you do about them is all up to you. Just don't say you haven't been warned."

The Preacherman

Male—20s

And then behold, there was one who came to him and said, "Master, what shall I do to be good so that I may have life everlasting?" And Jesus said, "Thou shall not steal or murder. Thou shall not bear false witness against thy neighbor. Honor thy father and mother. And love thy neighbor as thyself."

"I have kept the commandments," the young man said. "What more must I do?" And Jesus said to him, "If you wish to be perfect, sell all your worldly goods and give the money to the poor. Divest yourself of material things and you shall have a treasury in heaven." But when the young man heard what Jesus said, he bowed his head and walked sadly away, for he was owned by his many possessions and could not part with them. Not even to save his own soul.

I look at you, son, and I see a man in exactly the same condition. A man burdened with material things. A man weighed down and sinking by the gold around his neck and fingers and wrist. And I say to you, son, what the Lord said to that young man so many centuries ago. "Give me the ring, give me that gold watch and chain. Give me the money in your wallet and the credit cards, too. Give me what you have in the bank and a percentage of that weekly paycheck you have coming in. That money will go to the poor and toward repairing the church, which is the house of God. That money will shelter the homeless and buy medicine for the sick. What higher purpose can money be used for than the things I just mentioned? Think about it. And while you're doing that, let me look at the ring and the watch and the gold chain. I'll give them back, of course, but just for a moment, let me look at them please."

I look at these things and I see the weights that will sink your soul. And I know that it is my duty to relieve you of them. . . . I know I look young and I am young. And I know that you're asking yourself how a man so young can know anything about any of this. But I say to you, my son, the Lord works in mysterious ways. . . . He chose me as His servant and it is not for us to ask or question why. We only serve the Lord and obey His wishes. The Kingdom of Heaven is closer than we think. All we have to do is reach for it. And that's what I'm here to do. Help you to reach for it. The first step is the rings . . . Thanks. . . . Then the gold chain. . . . Thanks. . . . Now the wallet and those credit cards. . . . Bless you, bless you, bless you. Now you're seeing the light. Now you're on your way to being saved.

An Almost Perfect World

Male—30s

There is a saying that goes: Women fall in love with their head and men fall in love with their eyes. I don't know if that's true or not because I ain't a woman. And since I am only one man, so I can't speak for the others, only myself. But sometimes I think something must be wrong with me because I fall in love all the time. Sometimes standing on a street corner, or in a restaurant, or in a line for the movies, or sometimes just shopping in the supermarket. You name the place, if there's women around and they're young and shapely and full of whatever it is that women have that make them move a certain way, smile a certain way, fix their hair a certain way, dress a certain way, you can bet your paycheck for a year that I'm going to fall in love.

Now maybe it won't be for long. Sometimes it's only for a minute, five minutes, ten minutes or so, while the woman is still on the elevator, or walking down the street and still in my sight. The minute she turn the corner and disappear or get off the elevator my mind turn to other things and all the love in my heart vanish just like that (*Snaps his fingers*) till some other sweet thing cross my line of vision and my heart start pumping fast again.

Now some people will tell me that's just lust. Lowdown lust at that. And yes, I'll admit, lust got a little bit to do with it. But it ain't all just lust because I don't just want to lay up with the women I see. I want to sit with them, talk to them over dinner and drinks, swim with them in a pool or on the beach, whisper a joke in their ear and watch them laugh at it, ride bicycles or exercise in a gym with them and a thousand, maybe two thousand other things. Yes, sex is definitely a part of the equation, but it ain't all of it. No sir, not by a long shot. I have romantic feelings I would like to exhibit toward these women if only one of them would come up and talk to me, hold my hand, or smile at me and tell me they're thinking about me the way I'm thinking about them. But that never happens. If our eyes do meet, they'll give me a quick half smile just to be polite. Some of them. Most just look straight at me like I ain't there and what they really looking at is the wall or the world that's going on behind me. In other words, I'm transparent. I don't exist. Or if I do, I'm in another dimension from theirs. So as far as they're concerned I might as well be invisible.

I see it on TV and in magazines all the time, women talking and asking, "Where are all the men? Old-fashioned men, romantic men, good hardworking men." Then they go on to say that these men are hard to find and that they go home lonely and depressed almost every night.

Well, all I got to say is, "Ladies, you looking in the wrong places and giving off all the wrong signals." Because I am here, I am available, and I ain't alone. There are hundreds of men like me out there. And you can expand that to thousands and even millions. And all of us don't go to single bars or hang out in sports clubs. You can find us all over. Riding the morning train, sitting at the counter in a coffee shop, or sometimes just waiting at the corner for the stoplight to change. The procedure from there is real simple. I'll look at you, you look at me. We'll both smile. I'll say, "Good morning," "good afternoon," "good evening," or whatever. You'll answer back in the same kind of way. I'll ask if you having a nice day and you'll ask the same thing of me. We'll walk together for a while and let things go where they naturally want to go. . . .

That's the formula and the way I see things in my head. But that's a movie, a dream, a fantasy. Now if I could only take that dream and turn it into a reality, then we would have an almost perfect world.

Living in Dorksville

Male—19

Now I was really looking forward to going away from home, checking into school, and getting into the dorm with a roommate, whoever he might be. When you been living at home as long as I have, under the pressure of my parents and stuff, believe me, the idea of escape and school and new friends and just hanging out on weekends is heaven. Pure, incredible heaven.

When I met this guy I was going to be living with, he told me his name was Barney. Hey, that's an okay name, Barney. I don't mind it. I don't like it, but I don't mind it. Said he was born and raised in Lubbock, Texas, and ever since he was a child he wanted to be an animal doctor. A veterinarian. That's what he wants to be. A veterinarian. Fine, cool, okay. Me? I don't know what I want to be except maybe a rap star, a million-dollar basketball player, a record company executive, and a late-night TV comic all rolled into one. But he wants to be a veterinarian. "Different strokes for different folks" is what I say. Man want to help mankind is fine. Me, I just want to help Numero Uno. Yeah . . .

We get back to the room and I tell this guy that I like to party and play bongo drums. "Bongo drums," he says. "Yeah, and other African drums, too. It's a heritage kinda thing, you know."

He said he understand but then he told me about his study habits. From eight to eleven at night he need it to be quiet because that's the time he studies. Three hours a night all week including Fridays. Three hours a night! What is this guy, some kind of social retard? Some kinda walking robot who don't know the facts of life? . . . So I said to him, "Hey man, this is college. Time to loosen up, baby. Time to play. Time to party and puke, then party some more. Time to let the chicks see what they been missing at home. And time to let them sample what the future has in store." "You like chicks?" I asked him. He said yes and that he had a girl at home he was planning to marry. Marry? At our age. What could I do with a guy like this? But before I could say any more, he said, "Excuse me, I have to study," and went over to his side of the room. That was nearly a month ago and things haven't changed for the better. If anything, they mighta gotten worse. I'm living in Dorksville with the Emperor of Dorksville, who wears glasses, never watches TV or listens to music, and studies all the time. Is this what I came to college for? No! Hell no!

So what am I going to do about it? I don't know. I mean, I got to stay in this room the whole semester before I can make a change. Want to know the honest truth? I don't know if I can last that long. I feel as if I'm flipping out already. Feel as if I'm going out of my gourd. All kinds of crazy things keeps passing through my mind. Like maybe I should join the Army or Marines. Those guys got to have more fun than I'm having here.

It's like I'm living with my parents all over again. Only with them things was a little looser. "Out of the frying pan and into the fire"—that's what college is to me so far.

I'm reaching out to you because I'm asking for help. I'm like a man in the middle of the ocean drowning. Send me a life raft please. I'm begging you on my hands and knees, please, please, please get me out of here.

A Warning

Male—mid to late 40s

When's the last time you said you eat? Two days! Damn, no wonder you trying to gobble that hot coffee. You must be a fool, boy. A fool or a goddamned idiot. Anybody who don't eat for two days got to be one or the other. Ain't no in-between either.

Here. (*Gives him a plate of food*) Now don't eat that too fast, else you get yourself sick and ain't no use to nobody.

Had us a boy like you here years ago. A boy named Pete. He come in here looking for a job and was hungry, too. So damn hungry that when I give him food he damn near choke hisself trying to get it down in his stomach. Had to tell him, "Slow up, settle down." When he was finished, that boy was so grateful he damn near kissed me. Months later it turned out that he was a no-good, thieving piece of black trash. Couldn't put nothing down without that little bastard trying to put his hand on it. Hope you ain't like that. Hope you ain't like that at all. Because if you is you ain't going to last long in this job. Plus if I catch you stealing I'm gonna try and kick your behind somewhere southa the North Pole.

One more piece of advice I got for you. I wouldn't stay here in this job too long if I was you. Two, three weeks, and I'd be moving on. This place ain't healthy. It ain't got nothing for a young boy like you. Nope, it ain't got nothing at all. See all them bums and derelicts you pass when you come in? All them winos and losers? That's what the whole population of this area is. Deadbeats and lost souls, all waiting to die. And if the Lord is merciful, he'll do it quick. So you don't want to be in a place like this for long. Cause if you stay you gon' wind up just like them one a these days.

And this coffee shop ain't nothing either. Just a run-down diner in the middle a nowhere.

There used to be a lot of old buildings in this area but the city knocked them down and didn't bother to build nothing to replace them. So this whole area is just one big garbage dump for the city. Which is why we have so many rats all over the place.

So, what I'm saying, boy, is that there ain't no money to be made hanging round here. Only thing you gon' get is misery and more misery and more misery on top of that. The woman that own this place is a miserable witch, and she got a daughter more miserable than her. Them's the people you gon' be working for. You got the choice. You can listen to me or you can fall into the same trap that I did years ago. But if you do, don't say I didn't warn you.

.

Wondering Out Loud

Male—over 50

Sometimes a woman can affect you like that. I go into the place for a drink almost every day after work. Sometimes that boy I work with is with me. But most of the time I'm by myself. I wave at Vonde, who own the place, if he's around, say hello to Bobby the barman, and take my usual little table out on the porch. Bobby brings my drink, we chat for a little bit, and then he go back behind the bar. So I sit there looking at the world, thinking about life, and that's when she come by wearing them cutoffs that girls like so much, carrying a load of wet laundry to hang out in the sun. She see me and she wave and she got to know that she putting all kinds of bad thoughts in my mind. Thoughts that gon' keep me up at night and then put me to sleep with a dream and a smile.

Her name is Sonia and she can't be more'n twenty-three or twenty-four. And everything about her is perfect from the color of her skin to the way her hair fall round the back of her neck. And them legs. Oh man, I don't even want to think about them legs, all bronze and ebony and beautiful.

She hanging them clothes, stretching herself in all kinds of ways, and all I want to do is run down there and grab her. Grab her and squeeze her in all kinds of ways, if you know what I mean. But I can't. The girl is married. Married to Vonde who own the place. Vonde who weighs damn near 230 pounds. And who is at least three years older than I am. How'd that man get so lucky? I have no idea. All I know is after owning this place for damn near ten years he just up and decided that he needed a vacation. Didn't tell nobody where he was going. Left the fat old woman, Myrtle, he was living with in charge a the place. When he come back three weeks later, he had this girl, Sonia, with him, telling people she was his wife. "I fell in love and I got married," he said. Then he told Myrtle to pack up her stuff, take some money from the safe, and move out. "You don't live here anymore. So I want you to go."

Now if you know Vonde the way I do and like Myrtle does, you know that Vonde ain't a man to argue with. Vonde is a man who live outside the law and don't care about other people laws either. So Myrtle did as she was told and that was it. She was gone and this young girl Sonia was in.

They been together now close to two years, and that girl don't look like she want to go anywhere too soon. And Vonde look like a man who's content with life at last. And hell, who wouldn't be content having a young sweet thing like that tucking them in bed every night?

My problem is I want me one like that. Somebody sweet and sexy and young as Sonia. Somebody as friendly and faithful as she is, too. But I know the dream is hopeless. Good luck like that only come along once in a lifetime. And Vonde is the one who got it. So I sit here and look and wonder, what did Vonde do that was so right, that I didn't do that was so wrong? What god did he please and what god did I piss off? I know that I'll never know. But still I can't help wondering. And every time I look at her, I find myself wondering more.

Performance Rights

DATE DUE